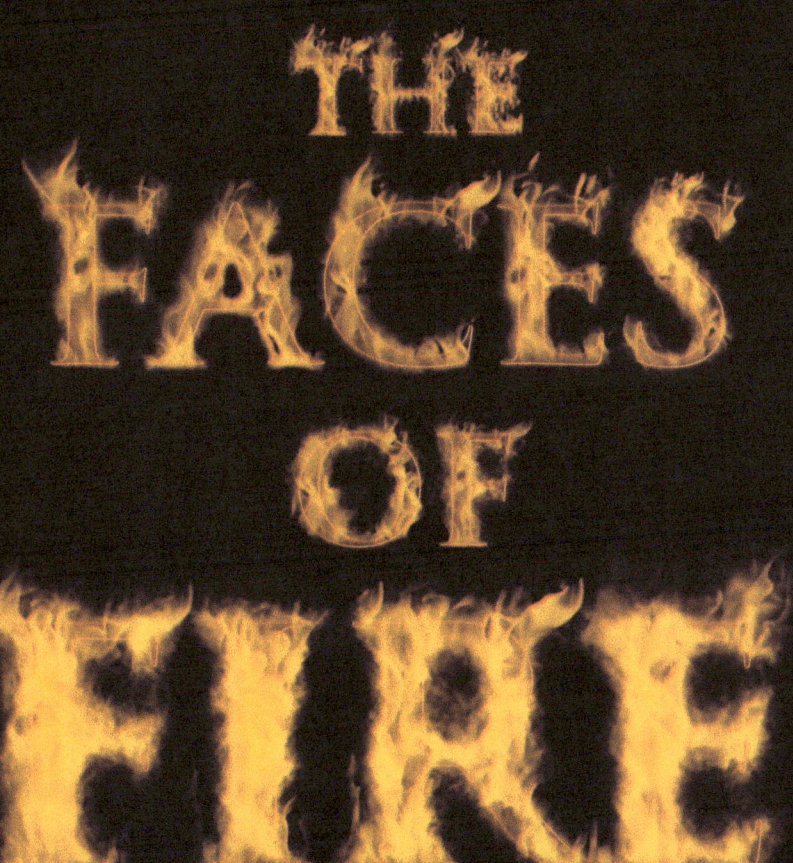

© 2019 Arminta Nelson. All rights reserved.

No part of this book may be reproduced, stored in a retrieval system, or transmitted by any means without the written permission of the author.

AuthorHouse™
1663 Liberty Drive
Bloomington, IN 47403
www.authorhouse.com
Phone: 1 (800) 839-8640

Because of the dynamic nature of the Internet, any web addresses or links contained in this book may have changed since publication and may no longer be valid. The views expressed in this work are solely those of the author and do not necessarily reflect the views of the publisher, and the publisher hereby disclaims any responsibility for them.

Any people depicted in stock imagery provided by Getty Images are models, and such images are being used for illustrative purposes only.
Certain stock imagery © Getty Images.

This book is printed on acid-free paper.

ISBN: 978-1-7283-3419-6 (sc)
ISBN: 978-1-7283-3418-9 (e)

Library of Congress Control Number: 2019917536

Print information available on the last page.

Published by AuthorHouse 10/31/2019

Dedication Page

I'd like to thank Ron Bowles for being so supportive of me, your friendship, generosity & artistic ability! This book wouldn't have happened without you!

I'd like to thank Joanie Stahl for being so supportive of me & being there for me through one of the hardest, most intense times of my life. Thank you for your friendship, mentorship & your prayers.

I'd like to thank Melinda Anthrop for all the bonfires, wonderful times & friendship. Without you this book may have never happened!

I'd like to thank Ed Moore for your crazy friendship & the pseudo bonfires.

I'd like to thank Lord God for everything, for my artistic ability & my peace. Without you I would be nothing & wouldn't have survived this life.

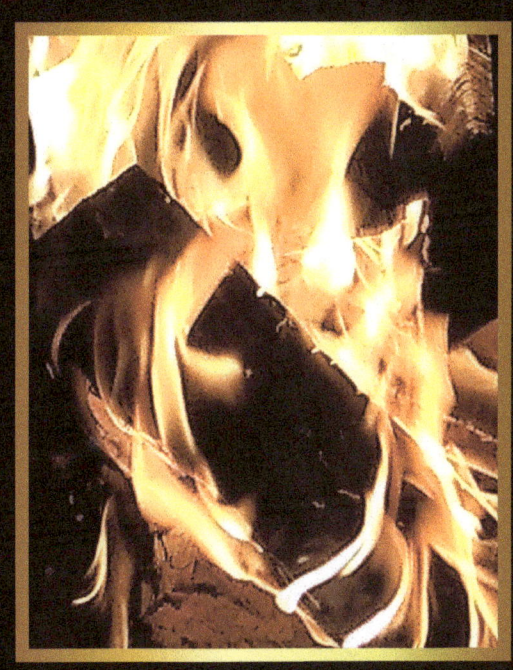
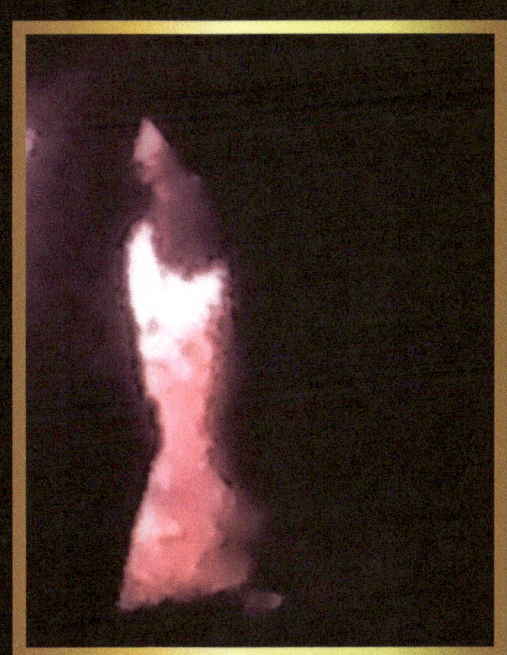
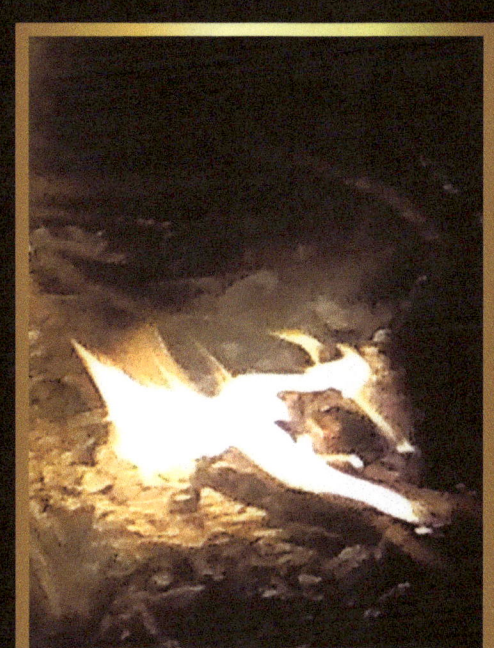

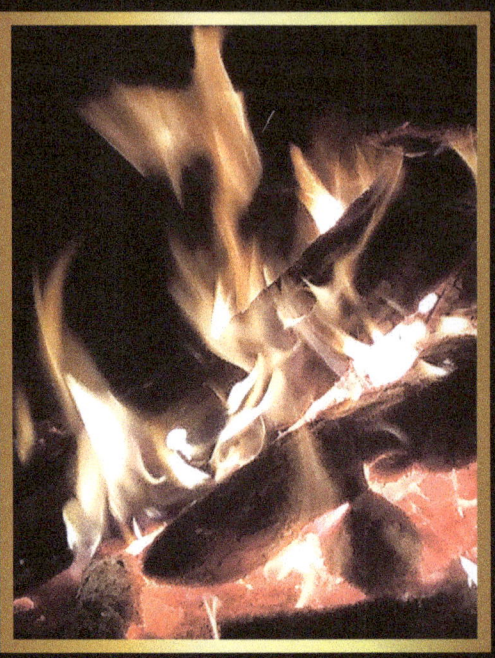
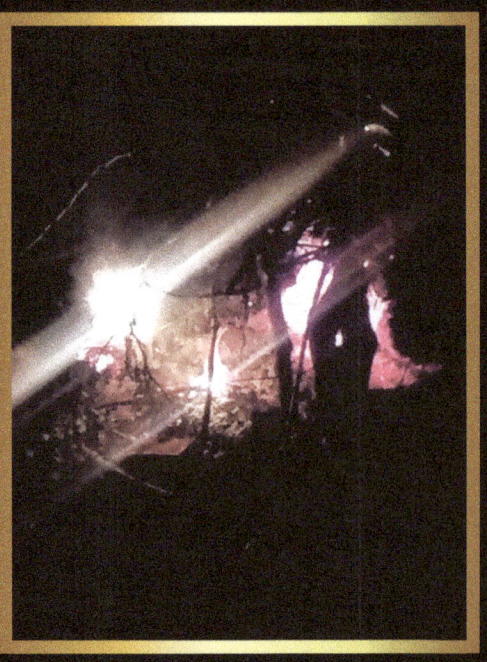
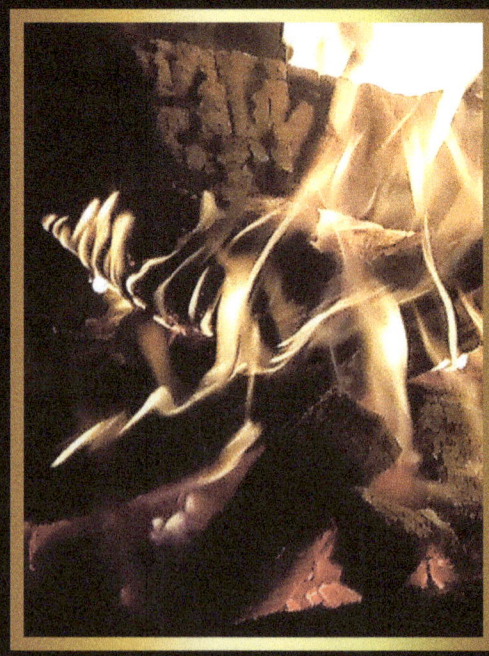

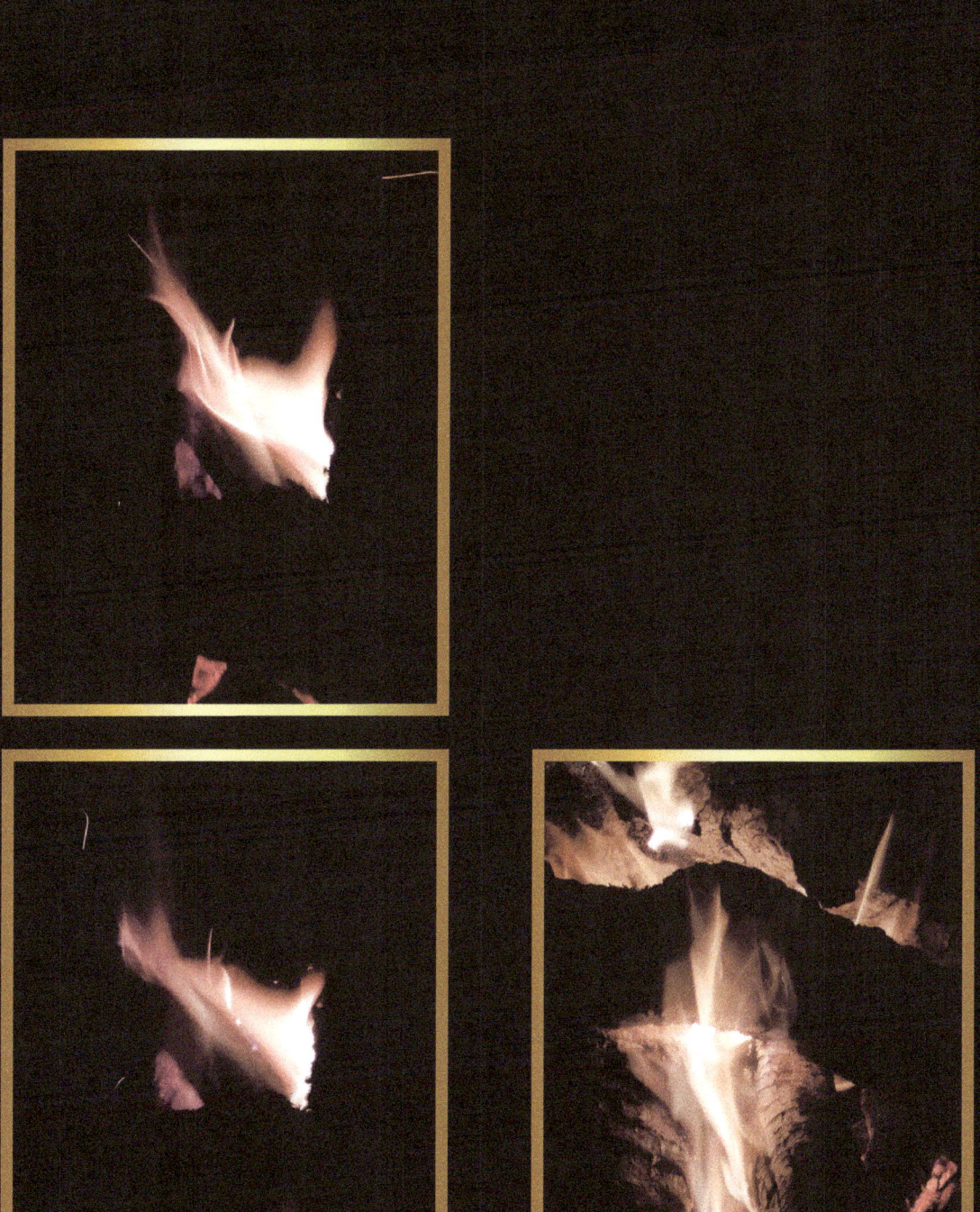

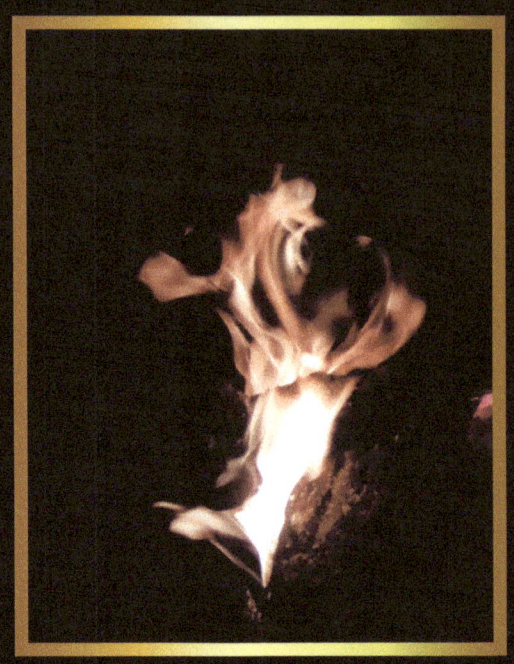
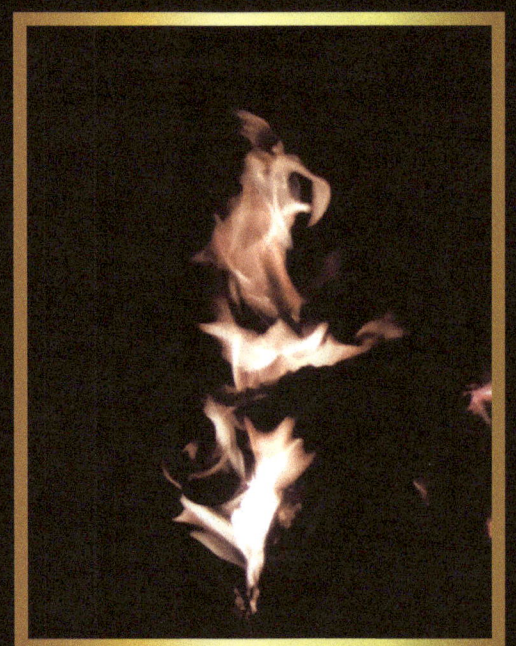
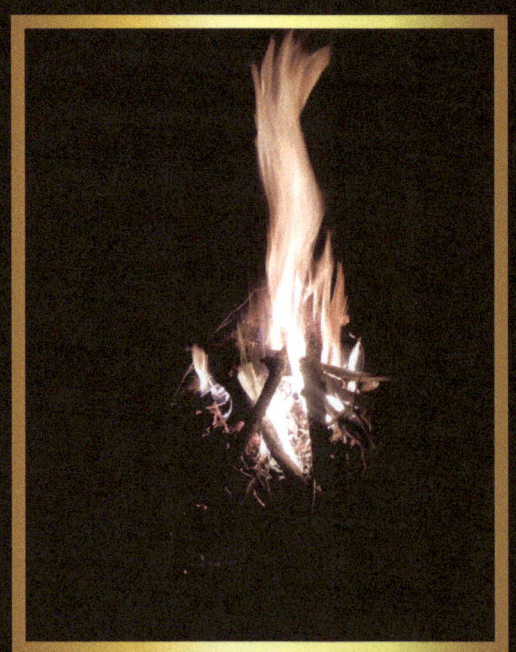

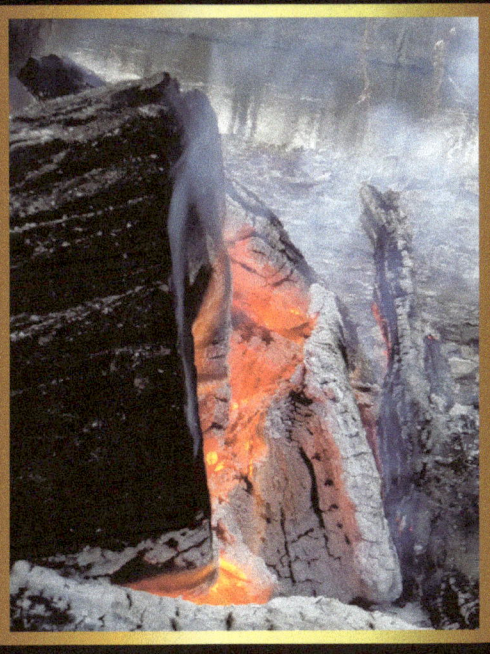
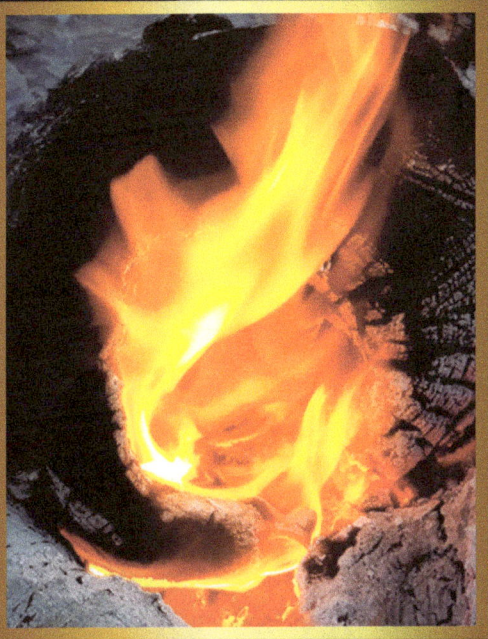
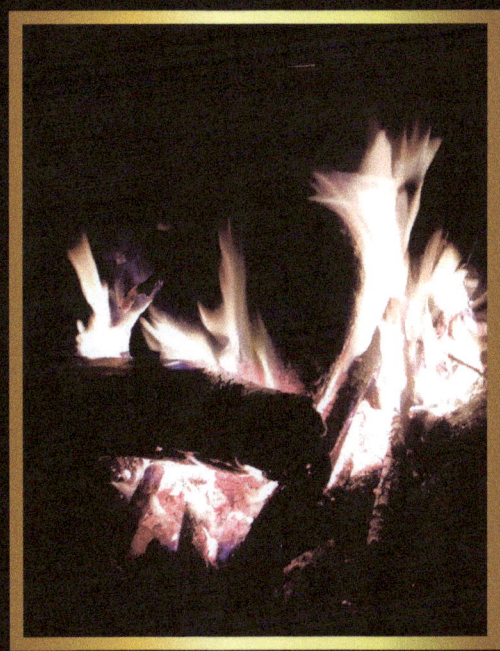

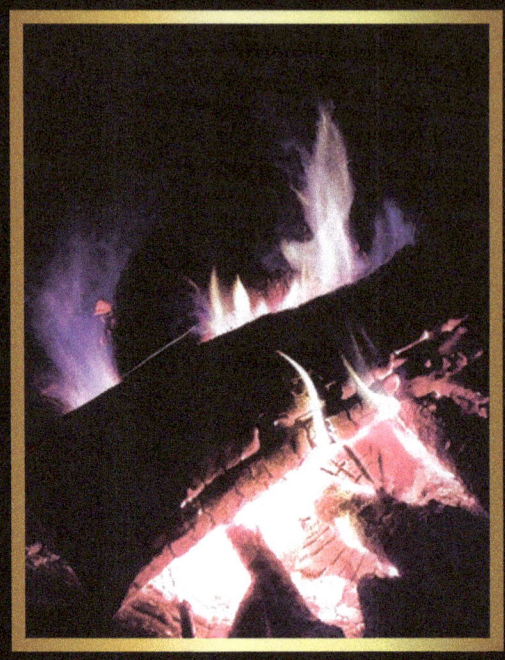
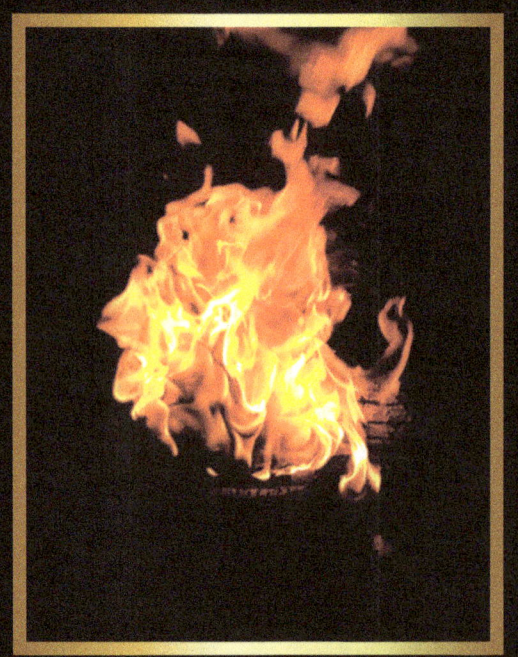
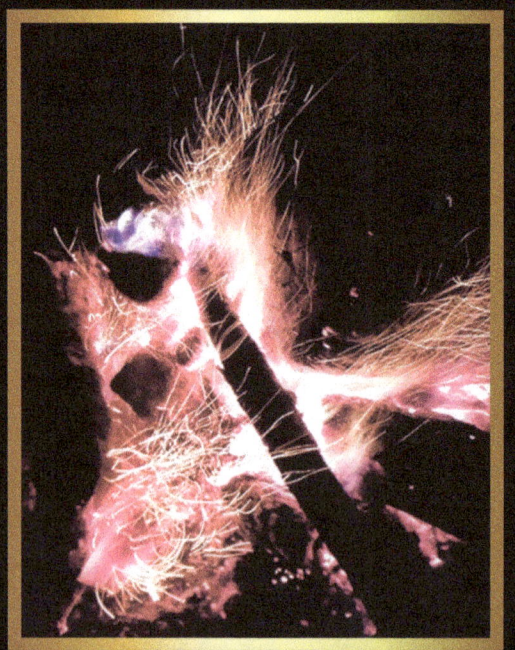

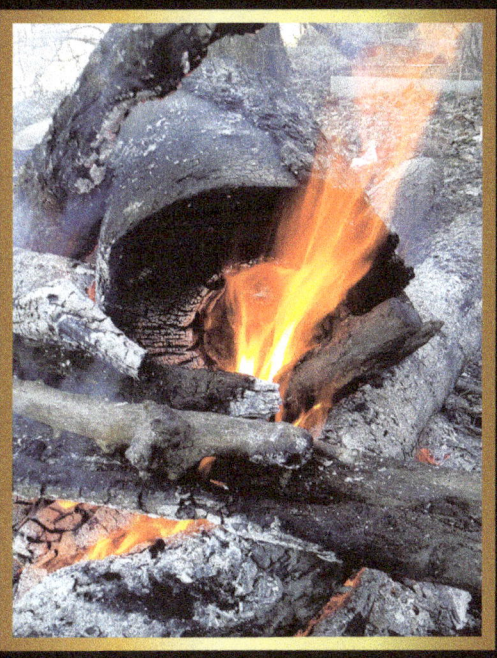
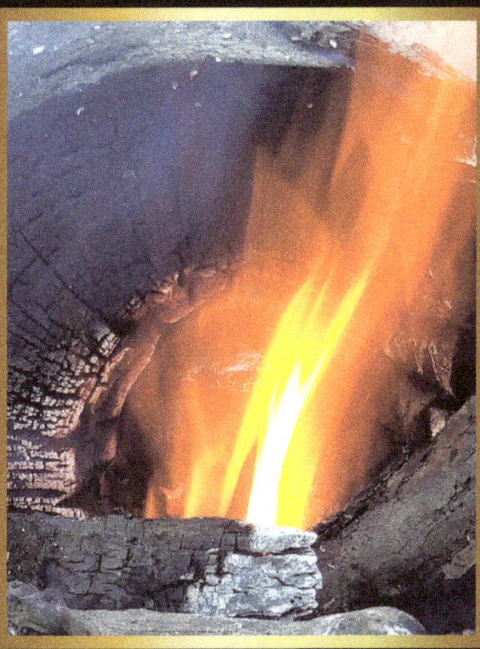
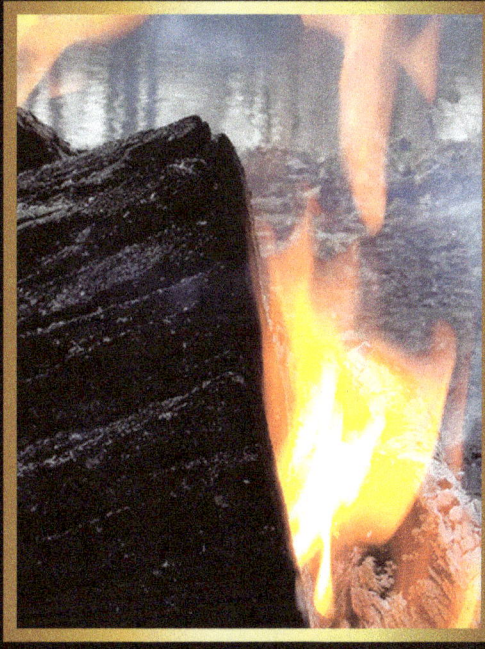

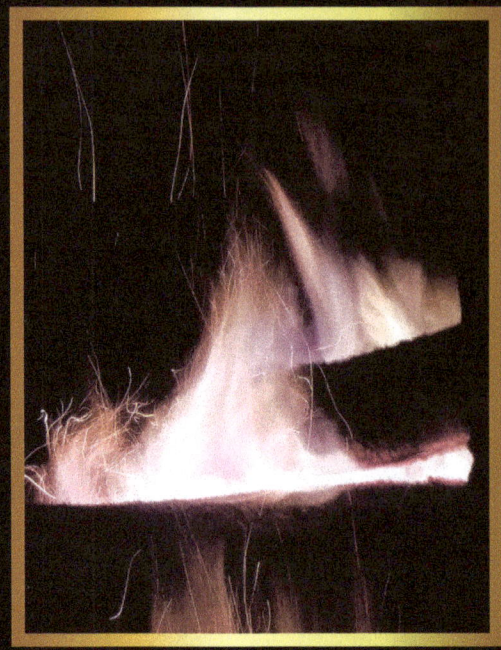
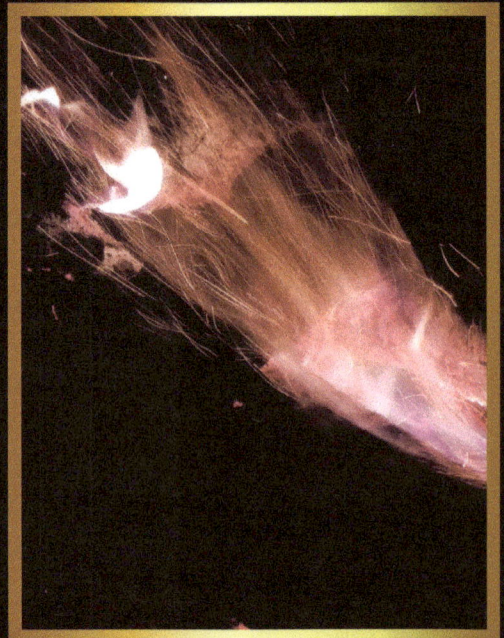
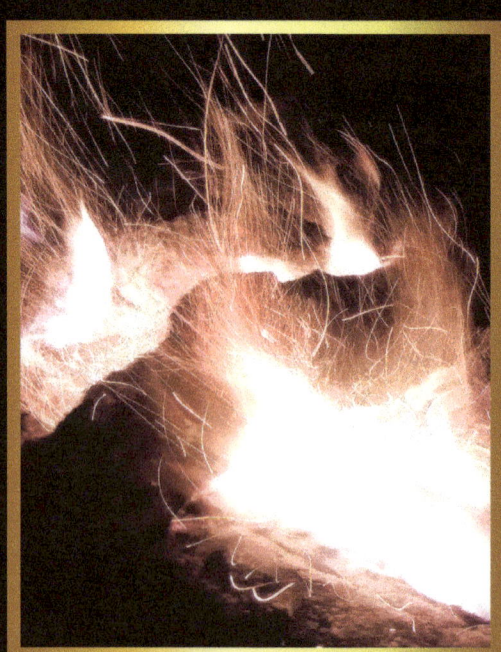

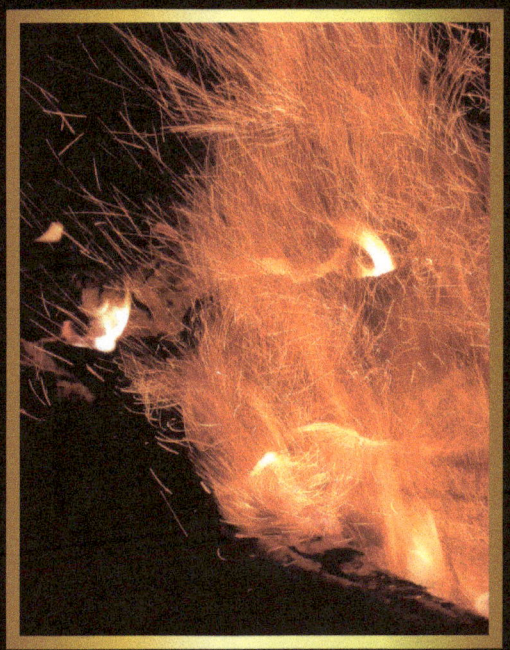
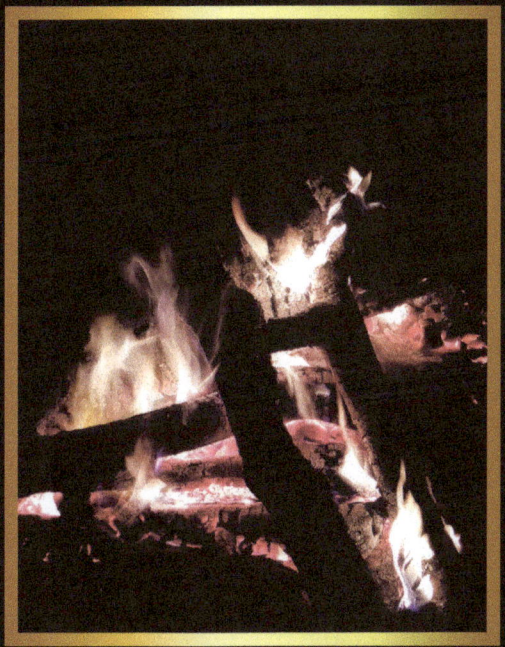
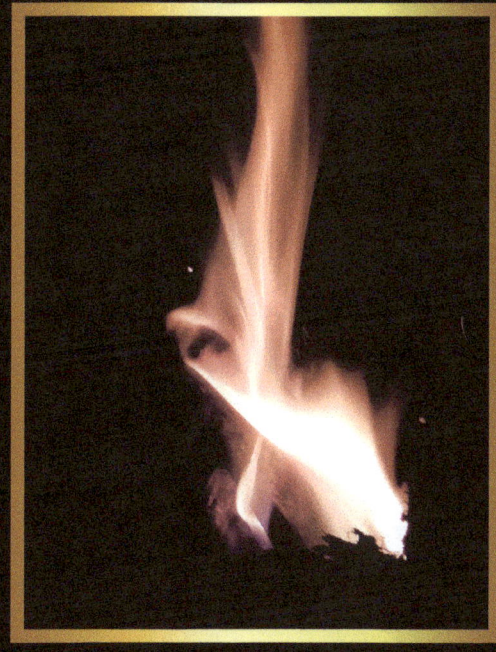

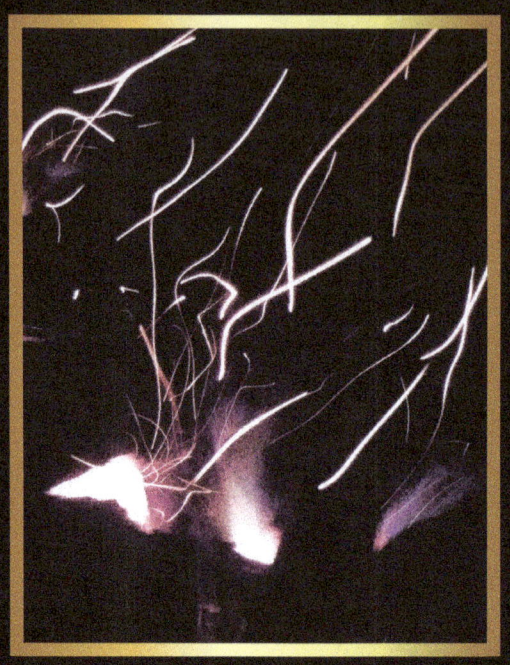
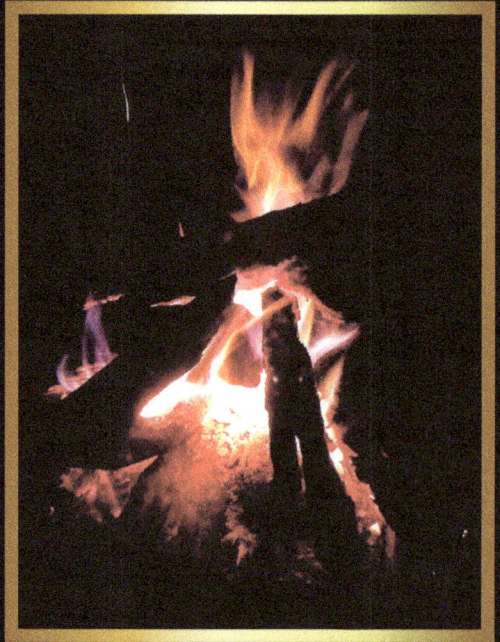
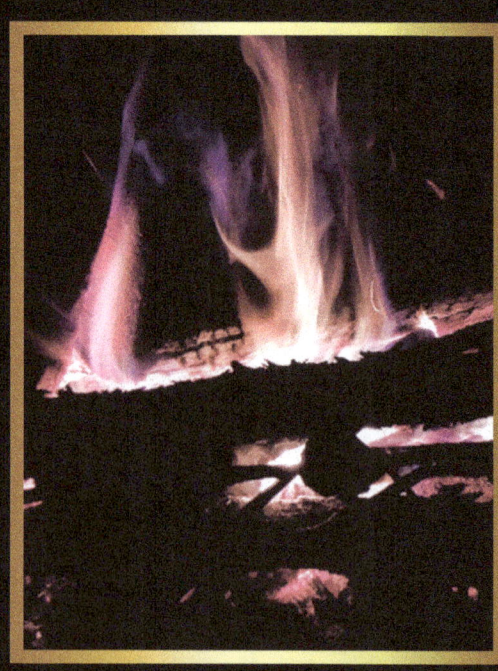

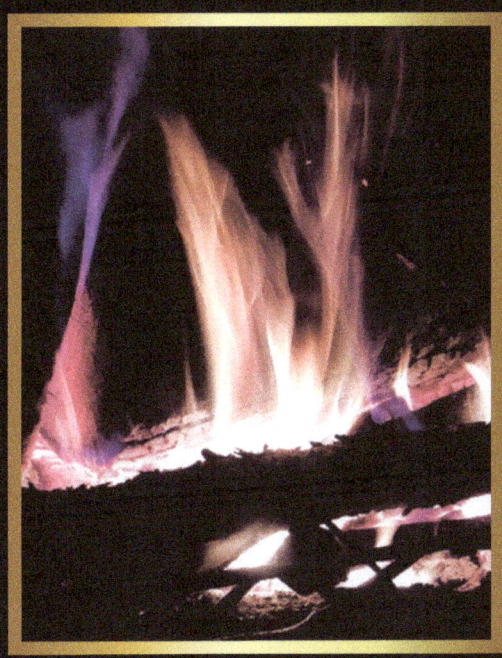
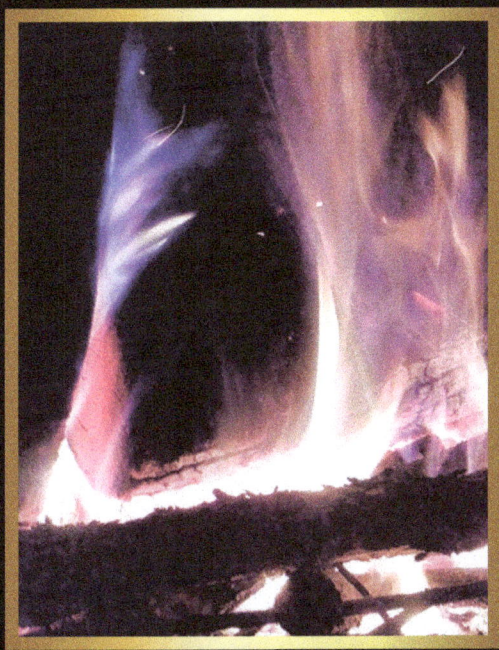
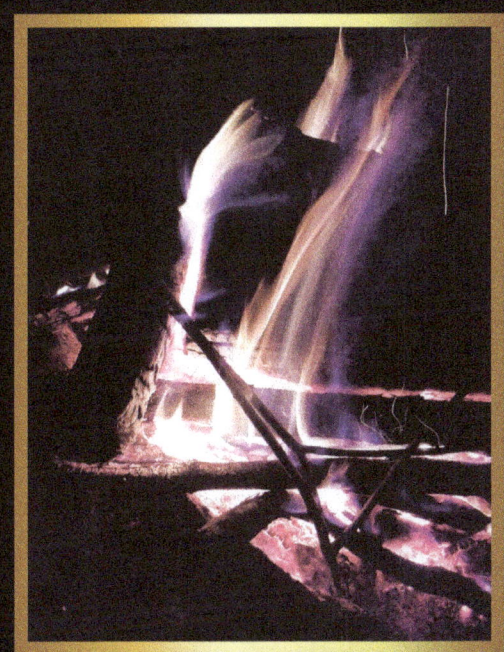

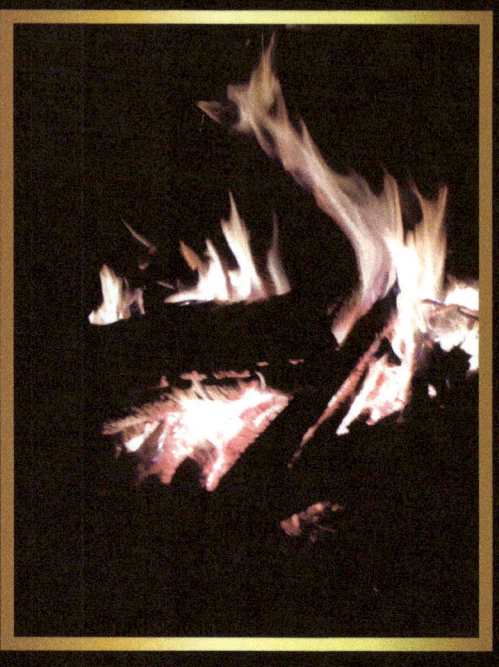
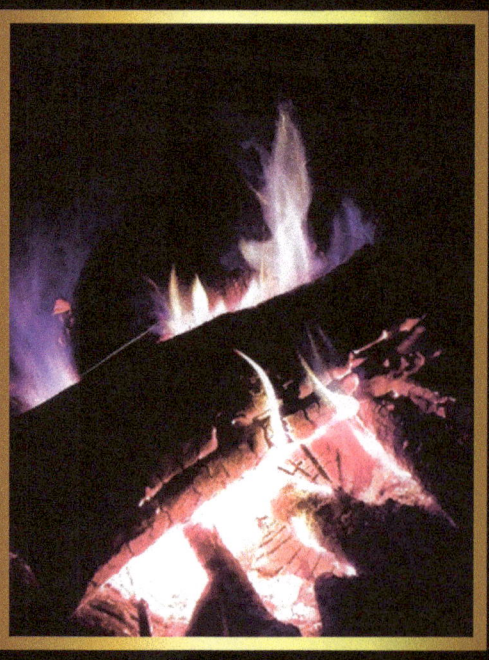
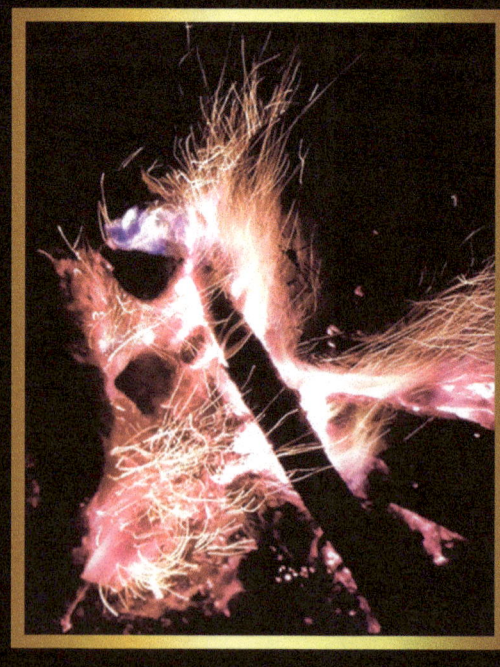

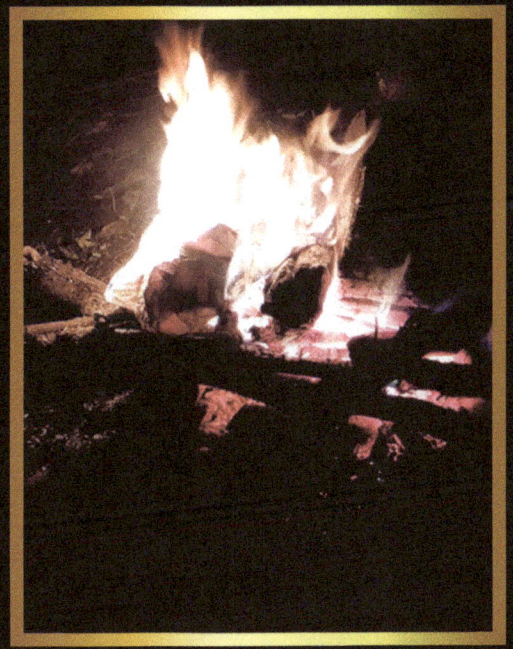
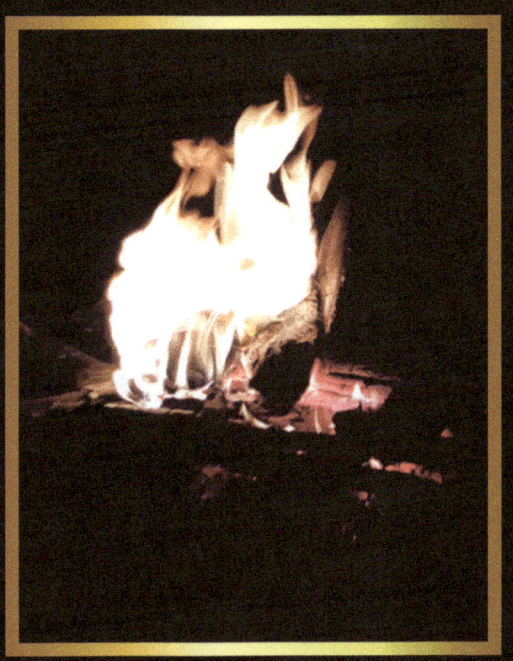
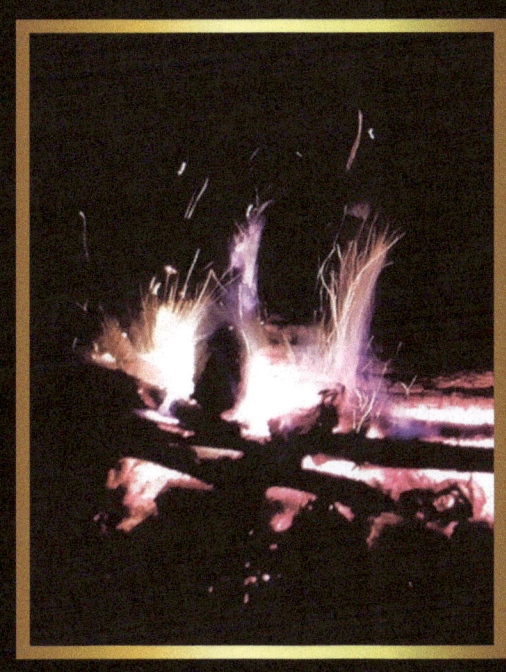

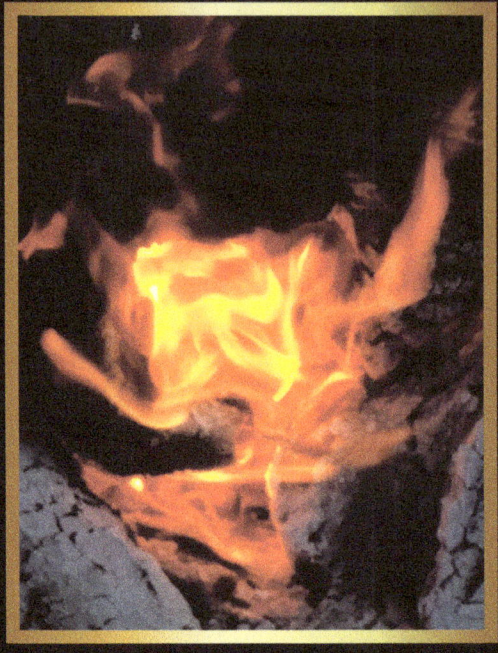
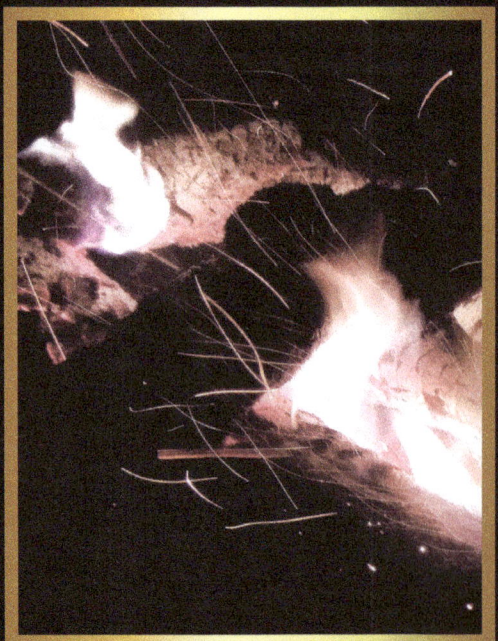
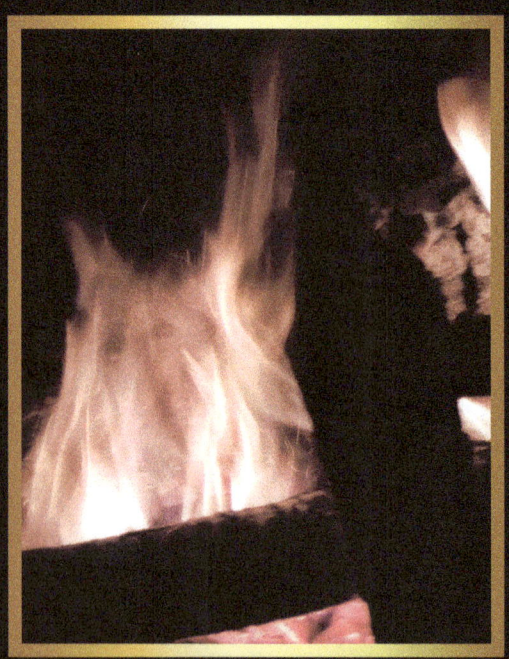

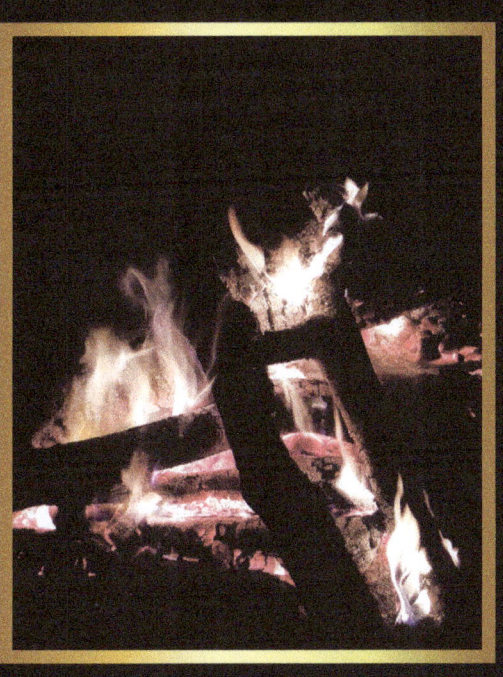
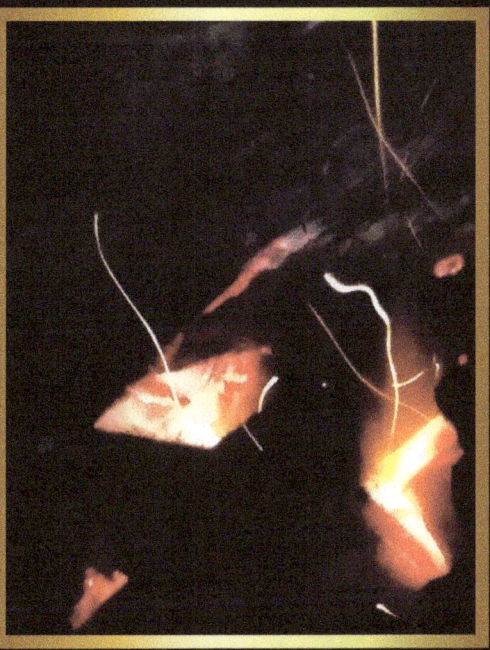
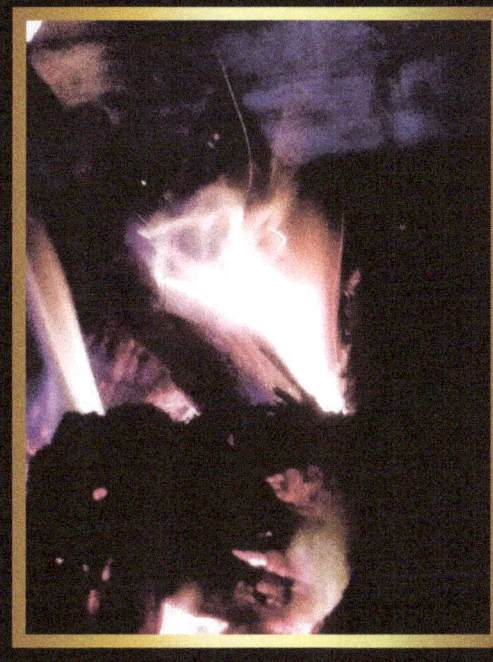

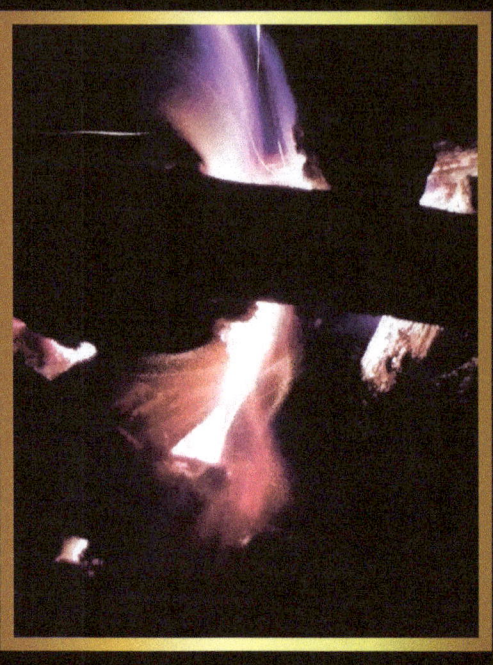
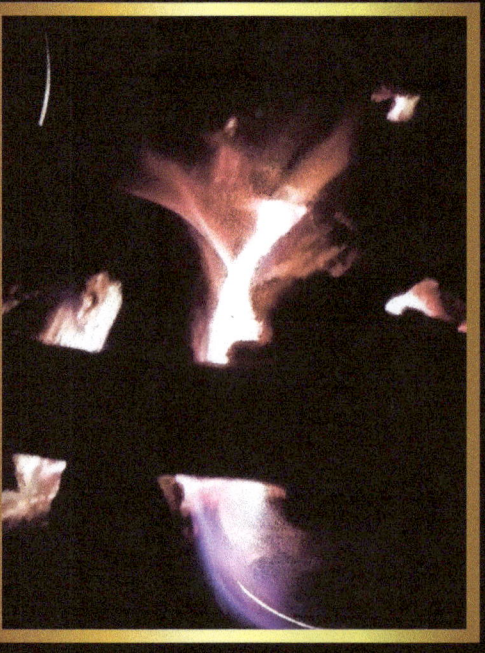
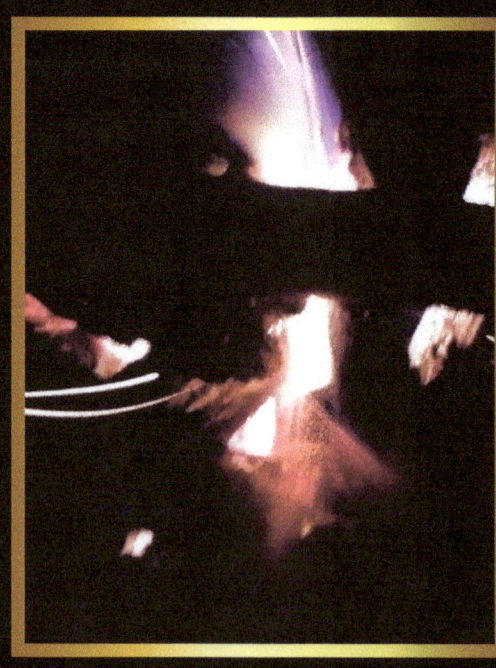

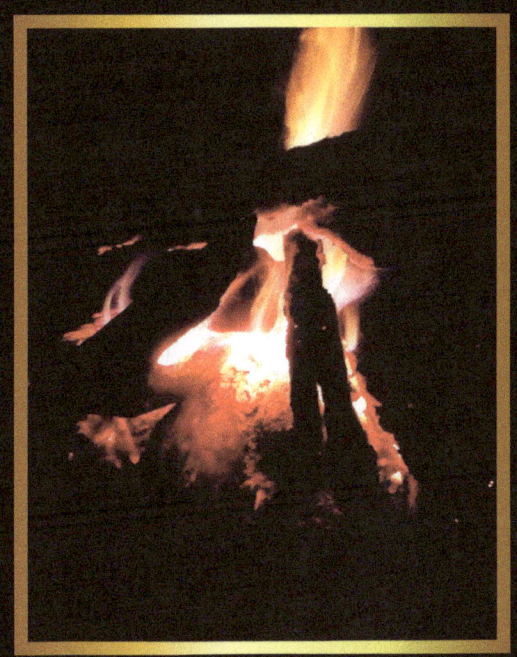
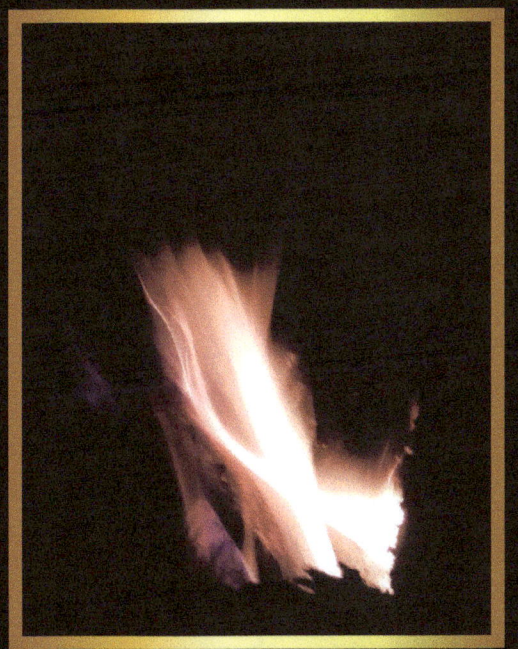
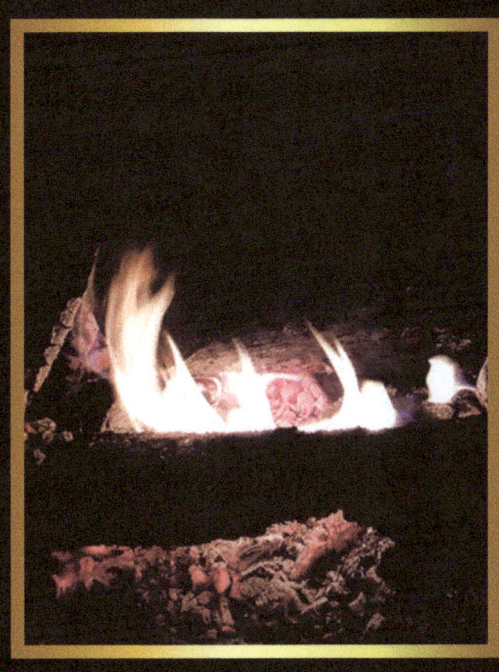

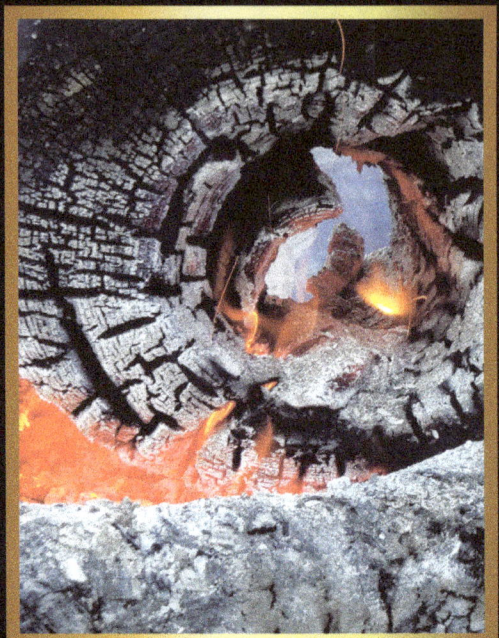
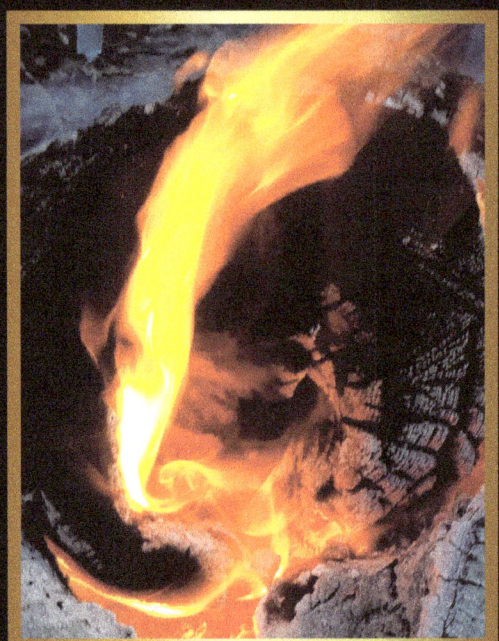
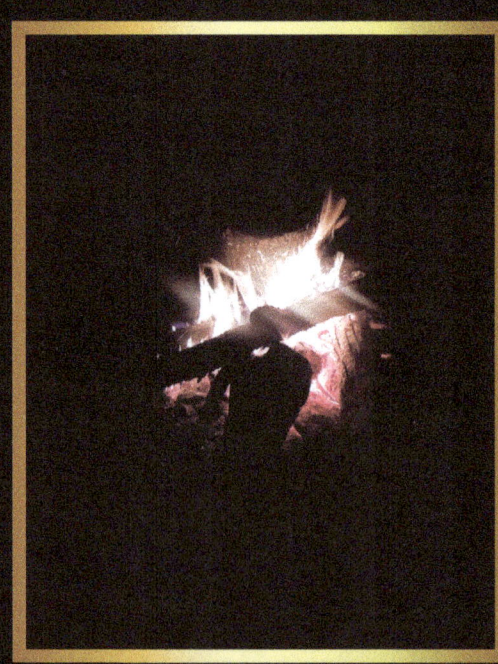

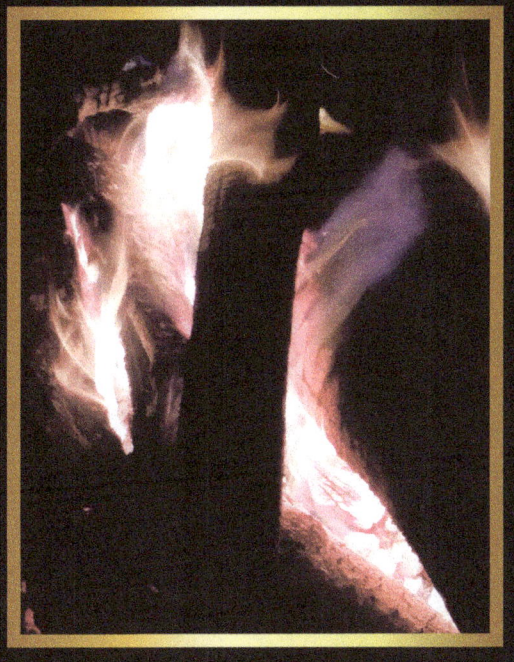
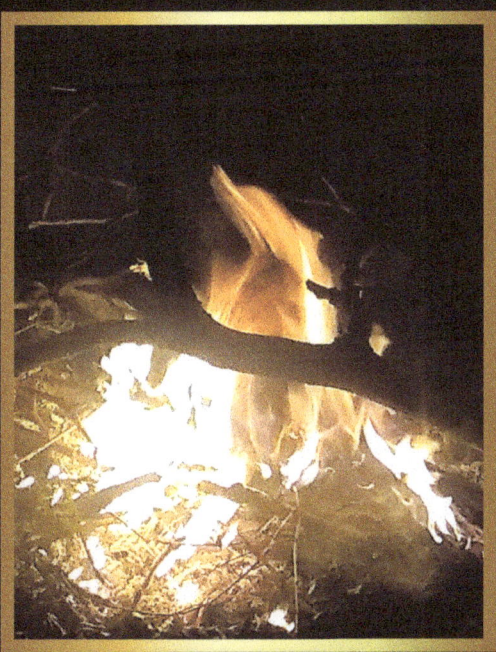
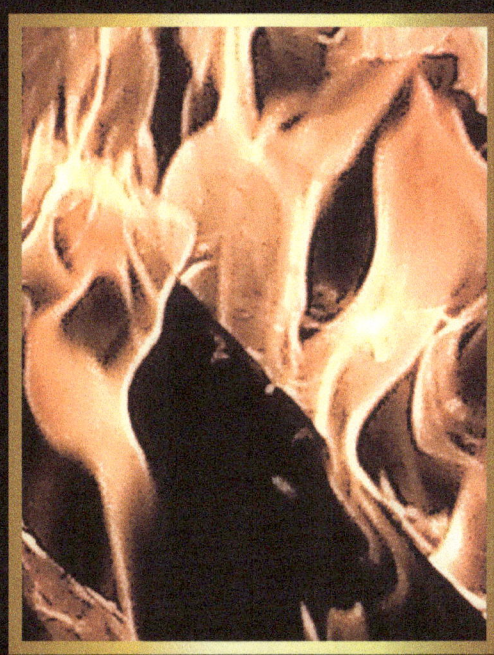

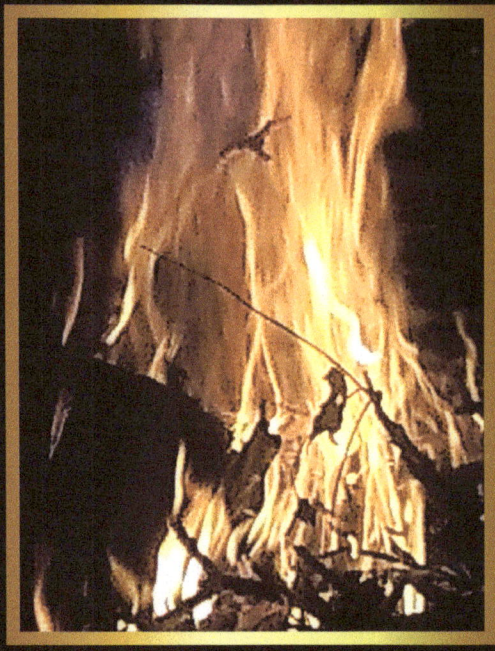
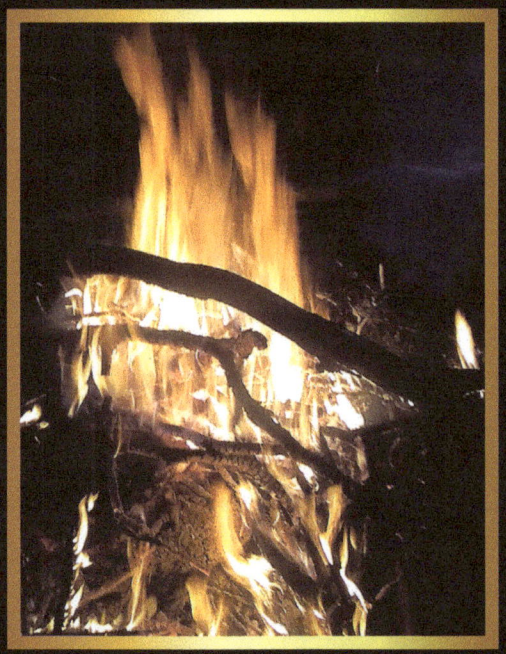
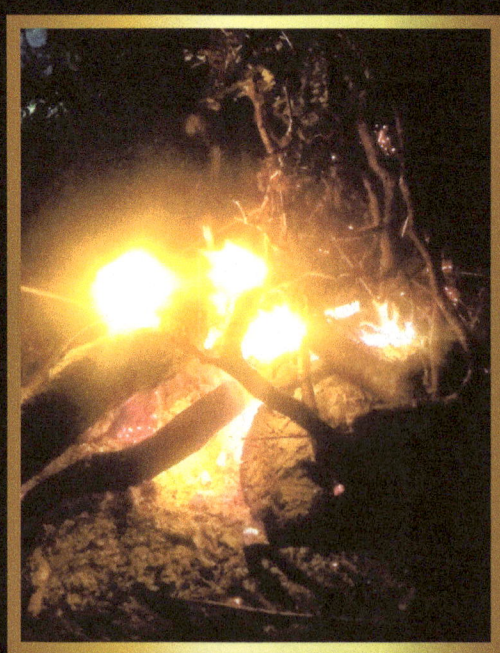

ABOUT THE AUTHOR

It has been really nice to finally focus on 1 of my artist abilities that I had always put off or kept in the background. I had always desired to actually move forward doing photography which I've loved since childhood.

Since I've recently started my life over, I'm not really doing anything with some of my other artistic talents which I've always focused on 1st so I needed to use one of my artistic abilities as therapy, which now is my photography. My greatest therapy has always been on stage as a lead singer & musician in a band. I've been a lead singer, musician, song writer, recording artist & dancer. Singing & performing live has been my passion & therapy expecting that would have really taken off. I hope that 1 day doing that again may happen but only time will tell, knowing it will happen in its own time.

One of my other creative endeavors is creating chic & unique Boho jewelry out of guitar picks.

Something that's been consistent throughout my entire life is being a professional driver. I've been an Over-the-Road Truck Driver, a bus driver, a limo & stretch limo driver, a shuttle bus & shuttle van driver & I've transported the disabled.

My artist endeavors have pretty much taken a back seat to driving.

Another thing I've done, in my younger days I was a competitive athlete, competing 1st in Physique Bodybuilding but changed to Women's Power Lifting.

www.ingramcontent.com/pod-product-compliance
Lightning Source LLC
Chambersburg PA
CBHW040545220526
45473CB00016B/3023